AMERICAN INDIANS SING

■ The American Indians had songs for everything that happened in their lives. In this book we will discover why and how the Indians made music and why these songs and ceremonies were so important to their lives and their daily living.

There were songs for good health, songs they believed would make the crops grow or the rain fall. There were songs to promote good hunting or bring the Indians into closer contact with the unseen spirit world. There were songs for war and peace.

The book describes the reasons for song in Indian life, introduces musical instruments and tells their significance, gives examples of the Indian's song-poetry, and emphasizes the importance of dance in ritual and ceremony. Specific ceremonies are illustrated and explained—the Sun Dance, False Face Society, Snake Ceremony, Green Corn Dance, Deer Dance and many others.

Most of the songs are from a time when the Indian roamed the country, before the coming of other people. They have been forgotten today except by some of the old men of the tribes. The last part of the book tells about Indian songs, dances and ceremonials of today. The blending of past and present gives an over-all survey of the first singing Americans.

Photographs and drawings, and more than a dozen songs transcribed in notation are included in the book, and a recording of many songs is bound in at the end. There are also lists of readings and other recommended materials. The introduction is by Dr. Frederick J. Dockstader, Director, Museum of the American Indian, New York City.

CHARLES HOFMANN

AMERICAN INDIANS SING

Drawings by Nicholas Amorosi

The John Day Company ■ New York

PHOTOGRAPH CREDITS: Charles Hofmann Collection: 18, 21, 90; Museum of the American Indian, Heye Foundation: 40, 42, 51, 72, 75, 76, 77; Bureau of American Ethnology: 46, 78, 79, 80, 81, 82; American Museum of Natural History: 50, 57, 60, 64, 65, 66, 68, 69, 71, 85, 87, 88, 89; James Friar: 56.

The John Day Company, Inc., 62 West 45th Street, New York, N. Y. 10036.
Published on the same day in Canada by Longmans Canada Limited.

Library of Congress Catalogue Number: 67-14614
Printed in the United States of America
Edited by Betty Warner Dietz
Designed by Carl Smith

ACKNOWLEDGMENTS

■   Of the many persons and institutions who added to the creation of this book, the following must be mentioned:

DR. FREDERICK J. DOCKSTADER for his interest, for allowing the use of photographs from the collection of the Heye Foundation's Museum of the American Indian, and for his introduction to this book;

DR. STANLEY A. FREED, Associate Curator of North American Ethnology at the American Museum of Natural History, for allowing the study of various musical instruments in the Museum's collection, shown in this book;

NICHOLAS AMOROSI, whose art work and illustration have added so much to this book, and who used the American Museum of Natural History's collection as well as the Charles Hofmann collection as examples;

DAVID PELLER, a student at New York's High School of Music and Art, who made transcriptions of songs and melodies;

HENRIETTA YURCHENCO, DR. WILLARD RHODES, and DR. WILLIAM N. FENTON for allowing examples from their recorded collections to be used in the recording included in this book;

For the use of photographs—AMERICAN MUSEUM OF NATURAL HISTORY, MUSEUM OF THE AMERICAN INDIAN, and BUREAU OF AMERICAN ETHNOLOGY of the SMITHSONIAN INSTITUTION, the last also for permitting quotations from various Bureau bulletins;

JAMES FRIAR, who in 1965 at age fourteen, photographed the Sun Dance Ceremony at Pine Ridge, South Dakota;

BILL and LOU GILLERAN, my young neighbors, who read the manuscript to me and criticized it;

lower grades of ST. HILDA'S and ST. HUGH'S Schools in New York City, where much of the material in this book was demonstrated;

MOSES ASCH of FOLKWAYS RECORDS for his encouragement and assistance in various projects through the years devoted to this study of American Indian music;

MAX SCHAFFNER, SIDNEY BAIMAN, and DENISE ASSANTE for assistance in many ways during the writing of this book;

DR. BETTY WARNER DIETZ, my editor, for her assistance and encouragement, valuable criticism, and especially her enthusiasm;

and

those *first singing Americans,* who made this book possible from the very beginning.

CONTENTS

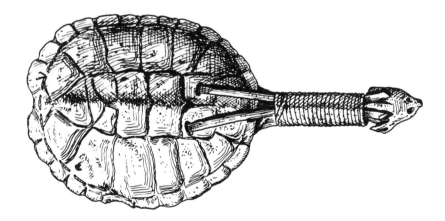

INTRODUCTION

■   Most studies of the American Indians in years past have been devoted to languages, social customs, history, and to collections of artifacts, especially handiwork. One of the great gaps in almost all these studies has been a consideration of oral literature, the dance, and music. Spoken poetry and folk tales have to be heard, just as music must be heard, and for study, the dance should be photographed in action. Motion pictures and tape recordings have come into their own only in recent years, even though Jesse Walter Fewkes was making recordings of Indian songs as early as 1890. A new interest in Indian music has resulted from the development of good field equipment. The exciting possibilities of its use have created an ever-growing audience.

The present book is an attempt to make available to younger readers an introduction to this world of song and ceremonial life and to demonstrate some of the wealth of culture possessed by the Indians. An actual recording of Indian music from seven different tribes is included to demonstrate something of the variety in musical expression of the first Americans. That all this music was soothing, as we understand the word today, certainly is not true; but neither is much of our own music that is heard today. These songs answered the Indians' need for musical expression, as true yesterday as today. The Indian sang for much the same reasons we do: for fun, for courting his mate, for worshipping his God. All of these needs must find expression in some vocal form, and this was as deeply enjoyed by the Indian as by any other group of peoples.

There is a wide variety of sound in the collection of melodies in this book. As an enrichment for a social studies program, this book will certainly strengthen the usual fare available for people interested in the Indian. This book, however, goes further in that it can be used to acquaint today's readers with the world of the Indian and perhaps widen their horizons as to what still remains of this culture. It must be understood that this is not a dead subject: one of the surprising survivals in Indian culture has been the vitality of language and music.

In presenting this material to the reader, Charles Hofmann has made available a wide range of Indian song and ceremonial from his long experience in teaching and working with Indian subjects. It is hoped that his work will introduce the reader to an even greater awareness of human musical response.

DR. FREDERICK J. DOCKSTADER

Director, Museum of the American Indian

Heye Foundation

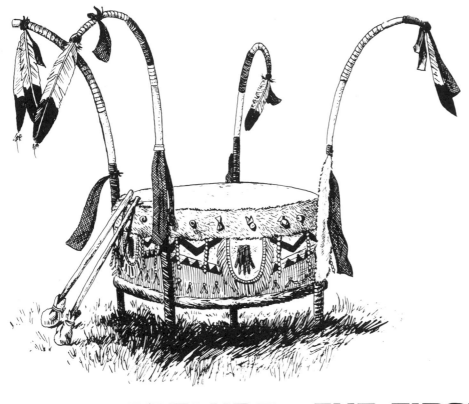

PRELUDE – THE FIRST SINGING AMERICANS

■   People all over the world like to sing. Some sing for fun. Some sing for very serious reasons — for prayer or to pay honor to an important person. There are songs for work and play, lullabies, wedding chants, and funeral dirges. Other people sing while they dance. There is always singing while one takes part in a ceremony or ritual.

For a long time certain of the world's peoples have sung for special reasons. The American Indians are a good example. In the old days men of the tribes had songs for good health, songs they believed would make the crops grow or the rain fall, and songs to promote good hunting. There were also songs for war and peace.

The American Indians had songs for everything that happened in their lives. In this book we will discover both why and how the Indians made music and why these songs and ceremonies were so very important in all their lives and in their daily living.

Most of the material in this book is connected with a time when the Indians roamed the country before the coming of other people. The songs were known and sung across the frontiers in the early days of America. Most of the songs have been forgotten today, or remembered only by some of the old men. The last pages of the book will tell you about Indian songs, dances, and ceremonials today.

The first part of the book (especially the first four chapters) deals with Indians and

Indian music generally. In these chapters, the typical or obvious characteristics of the songs and ceremonies are illustrated and explained. The remainder of the book deals with specific ceremonies, how they came about, and how they were used.

Blending past and present gives an overall survey of the first singing Americans.

■ On the title page of this book, you will find a pictorial map of our country which points out the location of some of the Indian nations and their ceremonials. Today there are about 200 tribes and over 400,000 Indians in our country. Therefore, only a small portion of these peoples' tradition and culture could be presented in this book. Individual books have been devoted to various sections of the country where one finds Indians of diverse ways of living and culture. Here are some of the areas and a list of many of the important tribes.

NORTHEAST (*from Maine to Minnesota*)
    Iroquois (*Seneca, Cayuga, Onondaga, Oneida, Mohawk*)
    Ojibway (*called Chippewa*)

Winnebago	Assiniboin
Menominee	Kickapoo
Sauk Fox	Shawnee
Delaware	Penobscot

SOUTHEAST (*Alabama, North Carolina, Mississippi, Florida*)

Creek	Choctaw
Cherokee	Seminole
Chickasaw	

PLAINS (*Dakotas, Montana, Wyoming, Nebraska, Colorado,*
      Kansas, Oklahoma)

Sioux	Comanchee
Cheyenne	Blackfoot
Crow	Shoshoni
Omaha	Ute
Pawnee	Ponca
Arapaho	Mandan
Kiowa	Assiniboin
Osage	Hidatsa (Gros Vêntre)

GREAT BASIN (*Montana, Utah, California*)

Flathead	Nez Perce
Paiute	Shoshoni
Washo	Maidu
Pomo	Hupa

SOUTHWEST (*Arizona, New Mexico*)

Pueblos:

Hopi	Pohoaque
Acoma	Nambe
Laguna	Santa Clara
Zia	San Ildefonso
Santa Ana	San Juan
San Felipe	Taos
Santo Domingo	San Lorenzo
Cochiti	Sandia
Jemez	Isleta
Hano	Zuni

Others:

Navaho	Mohave
Apache (*Mescaleto, Jicarilla*)	Havasupai
Pima	Walapai
Papago	Maricopa
Yuma	

NORTHWEST (*Oregon, Washington*)

Quinault	Hupa
Makah	Yurok
Skokomish	Klamath
Lummi	Swinomish

The variety and diversity of the Indian nations scattered over our land for thousands of years will give you an idea of how complicated is the study of so many different cultures. You will find many differences as well as similarities, as you would among any group of nations closely settled in one area. Realize that all Indians are not alike — that each tribe had its own traditions, its own customs, a way of life very different from that of its neighbors. They are not really "Indians" (as Columbus thought), but the great nations of the Iroquois, Sioux, Hopi, Navaho, Cherokee, and many, many more, who came from other lands to settle in the New World. Here, through the centuries, they made a new life based on the conditions of their environment. Some stayed in one spot and became farmers; some traveled because they were hunters. Throughout their daily living the songs and ceremonials added strength and courage to their primitive existence, and as you read this book you will discover how important these things were to these great nations of aboriginal America.

CHARLES HOFMANN

AMERICAN INDIANS SING

Men are gathering to sing the songs.
If thou art a man, go thither!
Eagle men are gathering,
Feather men, Deerskin men,
Men of the fires!

FRANCIS LA FLESCHE
"The Osage Tribe: Rite of Vigil"

SINGING FOR A REASON

■ Long ago an old Indian said,

"Around us all our lives there were songs. From the beginning to the end of our lives our people sang and the drum sounded through forest and across the plains. From first to last, from the cradle to the grave, our people sang and listened. There was nothing good in our lives without these songs."

Why was all this so important to the Indian people? How did the Indians think about such songs?

First of all, the Indian people believed in the power of all living things. An eagle, a buffalo, a bear, or even a tree was thought to have some power because it was alive. The Indians believed in certain powerful spirits, too, such as the mythological Thunderbird that lived in the sky.

The Indians needed many things in their difficult way of life. With songs the Indians called on all the beings, seen and unseen, that they believed had certain powers to help in any thing that was needed in life. The songs asked the spirits' help, or the birds' or animals' help.

Therefore, when the Indians sang they were trying to accomplish something more than human. In songs they were asking for more than human power. And to the Indians

this "more than human power" was brought about through certain songs and ceremonials.

Some Indians believed that "when the Earth was newly created, then the first time came the songs." Many stories of the Indians' idea of creation and many myths about gods and other powerful beings are found among varied tribes.

Many Indians also believed that a powerful being had given the songs to the people. Some said that the songs were given so that the people could be "happy and noisy, that they should enjoy themselves." They said, "The Earth is alive, the dirt is alive. The songs and the dancing shake the Earth and charge it with life."

This is one way the Indians believed it all happened. Some said that the Creator actually sang the songs; in this way the people learned them. And the songs were remembered because the Indians taught them to their children generation after generation. The tribes believed that they grew strong when the songs and dances were part of a ceremony that was held at a certain time each year. At this time most of the people took part and often the ceremony lasted many days.

Some Indians also believed in the power of songs received in dreams. The songs of the medicine man — the Indian doctor — were often received in this manner. Before an Indian became a medicine man, he might have received healing powers through a dream that he had when young. Young Indians often were said to have received visions or messages from powerful, or supernatural, beings. These dream songs were always used for a good purpose, usually to heal the sick or to make war magic. The Indians who sang them used them for the purpose of making a better, happier, or healthier life for themselves and their people.

You will read more about the importance of the medicine men later. You will read how the Indian doctor also used more than mere songs, how he knew the use of certain plants, roots, and herbs for various illnesses.

Indians in many tribes had different ideas about the ways in which personal songs were received. Since they believed in the power of all living things, it would not have been unusual to hear an old Indian say, "The Creator sends an animal to a person in his dreams. The animal speaks to the dreamer, and the animal, perhaps the Ant (even the smallest has power!), gives only one kind of songs, the Ant-songs. It starts out by singing several songs to the man. Some other night it returns and sings some more. Thus, the Ant goes on until there is a group of songs, perhaps forty or fifty. Then the Ant says to the dreamer, 'It is all right now. You may go and sing the songs to the people!' But even after this the being comes back to him and gives him songs again and again until the Indian dies."

The Indian who had received such dream songs could not sing them until he was given permission. And no one else could sing those songs until they were given permission by the man who "owned" them. If the owner sang them, they were powerful. The power of the songs was lost when they were sung by anyone else, especially without permission. Since these songs were the personal property of the man who had dreamed them, no other person could sing them without payment. An Indian might trade a song for several sheep, some blankets, a good gun, or even a herd of horses. It all depended upon the use and the power of the song. Usually the song was not "sold" until the Indian felt he might not use it so successfully again.

There were also important songs praising a man's success or generosity. Dreamed songs and purchased songs were, in the Indians' minds, associated with the power of magic, but the songs of praise were *honor songs*. These included songs for a brave warrior, a mighty chieftain, a powerful medicine man, and a devoted friend.

Apart from songs belonging to individuals were the songs that were part of the ritual and ceremony of a tribe. In the stories of these ceremonies you will read how certain rituals were explained when powerful, or supernatural, beings brought them to the people. The Sacred Pipe, for example, was brought to the Dakota, or Sioux, Indians by the White Buffalo Maiden, who described the power of the Pipe and told how it should be used in many of the ceremonies of these Plains people. At the same time the White Buffalo Maiden brought these people a new "religion." You must remember that the Indians never thought of the term *religion*. All these things concerned with powerful objects and living things were to them "the way of life." For them the world and the universe were "One" and the sole purpose in Indian thought was to keep good order in that universe. The songs and ceremonies brought about definite results needed in the way of life. Some men in the old days knew several hundred different songs — personal songs and others that were sung by all of the tribe in ceremonies.

Indians sang them in unison, and most of the songs were accompanied by drumming. Rattles were, in the beginning, the property of medicine men and their sound was a kind of magic. Words also were very important in Indian songs, but very few words were used in any song. The Indians knew the *meaning* and the *use* of the song and only two or three key words told the whole story.

To understand something of the Indians' music, one must know the story, the background, and the purpose of each song. These songs surrounded the Indian life like an atmosphere and we must remember that nothing in this life was complete without songs. Songs were always sung in the same manner and had to be letter-perfect. These ritual songs were carefully learned, rehearsed, and then performed with accuracy.

An old Indian said, "The path between the Unseen Ones and man must be straight." The spirits, ancestors or powerful beings, were appealed to through song and ceremony, just as many peoples over the world appeal for needed things in prayers. The Indians believed that to make mistakes or perform without accuracy would make the appeal miscarry, and the desires of the people would not be granted. "Good singers" were those who sang with accuracy; hence, we describe a singer as "good" rather than "beautiful" in judging his performance. When their ceremonies, for whatever purpose, are performed and good results are obtained, the Indian people know that the Unseen Ones are pleased

and that the power of the songs and dances keeps the people and the tribe strong and everlastingly hopeful.

You will read of many songs and ceremonies in this book, but you must hear and listen to Indians singing in order to know more about their music. You may have heard them sing at a public gathering, or perhaps you have heard them on television or in the movies. Why don't you listen to a few of their songs that have been recorded? A few samples of these are included with this book. Then you will know that all Indian songs are not alike, as many people believe. And all is *not* whooping and crying. There is more music than noise! There is great variety in this music. You will discover that there are many tunes.

Let us listen carefully to this music. When you hear the Indian sing find out something about the song. Know *why* the Indian sings it and *what* it means to him. Remember that these songs are sung for a good reason, for something important to the singer and his tribe. After that you will begin to appreciate the Indians' songs and know that music is a key to the understanding of their life and culture.

THE SOUNDS OF DRUMS, RATTLES, AND FLUTES

■ The sound of the drum, rattle, and flute is old in this land. These instruments of the Indian people were heard in woodland and prairie, mountain and desert, when America was young. They are still heard today, even though only the old men of the tribes remember all the sounds.

So many things come to mind when we hear the beat of the drum. It is impossible to separate the drum from most of the Indians' music. The drum reminds us of the warpath when the tribes of the Great Plains sang and danced for victory. The buffalo hunters with their bows and arrows prayed for success with songs accompanied by the drums. Throughout the land the drumbeat was heard, across the prairies, out to the desert oasis of the Southwest. There the Indians of the Pueblos sang and danced for rain. The drumbeat excited certain rhythms that for the Indians were associated with the supernatural.

The drumbeat is very strong in the accompaniment of most songs. The melodies of Indian songs are short and simple. The rhythm is heavily accented and the drum is the pulse beat of most songs. Many Indians cannot sing without the rhythm of the drum or the rattle.

There are three important types of drum found among the American Indians. Small drums are held in the hand, there are drums large enough for several singers to sit around

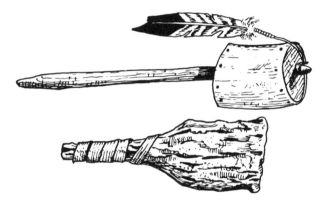

while drumming, and there is also an ancient type of water drum which could be heard for a long distance.

The materials used for musical instruments varied with the environments of the tribes. The Indian always used whatever was near at hand. Woods commonly used for these instruments included cedar, ash, box-elder, sumac, and hickory. Hazel, grapevine, and willow served as material for making drumsticks. Rattles were fashioned from gourds, turtle shells, deer hoofs, coconut shells, and other containers. It is not unusual to find rattles made of rawhide, pottery, and basketry.

Drums vary in size from the small 8- to 10-inch hand drum to a large specimen several feet in diameter, such as the Blackfoot ceremonial drum pictured, which may be played by several people at the same time. The hand drum may have one skin covering (like a tambourine) or a double head held by a loop fastened to the side. The tambourinelike single-headed hand drum is easier to hold and can be played while the singer is performing a dance, walking, or riding. A hand drum with one skin has a round frame, like a hoop, covered with rawhide, either fastened to the hoop or stretched so that the corners are crossed on the reverse side to use as a handhold. Often several men, each with his own hand drum, played together, especially at a large gathering. The drummers stood

in a row with the singers in the background and the dancers performed in front.

The large two-headed drum is made by stretching a skin over a section of log that has been hollowed out. Sizes vary from a height and diameter of from 1 to 3 feet. In later times one finds metal washtubs, wooden kegs, and other containers substituted for logs. A photograph from the Pueblo Indians illustrates this type. Note the heavy lacing of sinews.

Only one end of a log is hollowed for a water drum. Near the solid end a small hole is bored to allow water to escape. The large piece of skin which serves as the head is held tightly in place by a hoop. Water is placed in the opening; the head is dampened and then replaced. The water adds to the resonance. Most water drums are 18 inches or less in height. Recorded examples may be found in Iroquois' songs and those of certain societies. Often water drums are made from small iron kettles covered with skin.

Pottery drums and basket drums are not unusual. Both types are popular in the Southwest. Inverted half-gourds are also struck with small sticks.

Some colorful decoration is usually painted on the drumhead. Sometimes the decoration represents supernatural beings and is a symbol of something connected with the life of the Indian who painted it. Sometimes it is connected with the interests of the tribe, such as corn, rainclouds, or the power of the eagle, the turtle, Thunderbird, or buffalo. A medicine drum might be decorated with symbols of the owner's dream and his songs. Most of the time the decorations are simply the result of the Indian artist's imagination in making his instrument look beautiful.

A slender stick serves as a drumstick. There is usually a padded knob at one end. This knob is sometimes made by wrapping rags around the end of the stick, but in the old days skin was packed with softer material and tied in place.

Among some tribes the drumstick is regarded as sacred. It was often highly decorated with symbols. The designs were related to the cycle of songs for which it was used. Likewise, the drums were sometimes given high position. Some Pueblo drums were given names and lives in the villages as persons.

Rattles are found among all Indian tribes and there are many sizes and shapes. The rattle had magical significance and played a great part in the ceremonies of treatment for the sick. Since rhythm is associated in the Indians' mind with the supernatural, the rattle was another vital symbol for this belief.

The most common type of rattle consists of a hollow container filled with loose objects such as seeds, shells, pebbles, corn. The container most used is probably the gourd. Clay rattles are found in the Southwest. Rawhide globes filled with small stones are known among the Plains tribes. Woodland tribes used wooden boxes of birchbark filled with pebbles. Other types are made from buffalo or steer horns or turtle shells. All of these rattles are shaken by handles.

Other rattles were fastened to the dancers' legs below the knee or tied about the waist. Small turtle shells, cocoons, even pebbles tied in deerskin pouches, are attached to the body of the dancer during dances and ceremonials.

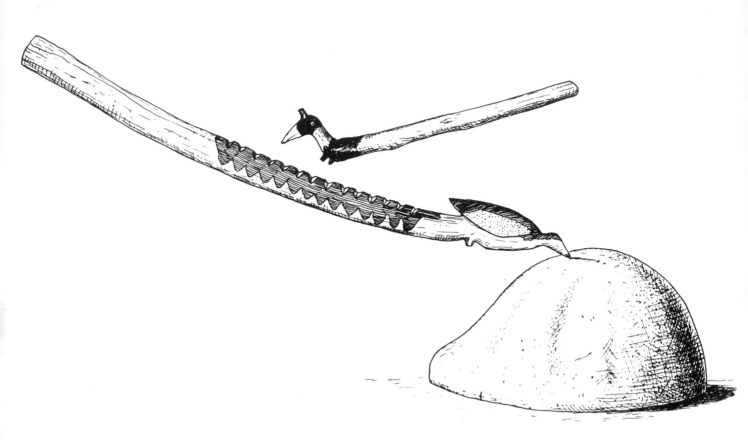

The notched resonator is a very primitive sound device. It is used over the world and many Indian tribes included it. The Spanish called it *morache*. Nowadays it is most popular in the Southwest. The player rubs a smooth stick back and forth over another stick or long bone which is notched. The notched stick or bone is sometimes placed on a drum, a dried half-gourd, or an inverted basket, which serves as a resonator. Listen to this instrument in recordings of the Yaqui Deer Dance.

Flutes and whistles were the two wind instruments among the American Indians. The flute was not known in ritual and ceremony except for the Flute Society songs of the Pueblos. Usually it is associated with the playing of love tunes and courting melodies. Here is a flute melody from the Chippewa of Minnesota.

A variation of this is found in the recording in the back of this book. American Indian flutes are played like recorders. They are vertical flutes that are sounded by blowing into an air chamber down a hollow tube. These tubes are from 1 to 2 inches in diameter and from 1 to 3 feet in length. The fingers of the player cover four or more open holes of the tube. These wind instruments are made of wood (cedar and sumac being popular) and sometimes metal (such as the barrel of a gun). Cane or bamboo also serves to make the hollow tube for a flute. Clay flutes are played in the Southwest.

The whistle is the property of medicine men and is used in treating the sick. It is also used in various ceremonies, such as the Sioux Sun Dance, and by members of war societies. The whistle produces a single shrill, high note. The best whistles are made from the wing bone of a bird. Some of these were highly decorated, especially with the feathers of an eagle. Medicine men's flutes seldom used such decorations. Long wooden whistles were heard in certain dances and served to make "courting calls."

A popular sound instrument found all over the world is known as the bull-roarer. Wherever it is known it seems to be connected with magic or the supernatural. It represents the voice of the wind or a spirit ancestor. You may have heard a similar instrument for Hallowe'en or on New Year's Eve. A long, stout cord is fastened to a flat piece of wood about 1 inch wide and less than 1 foot long. This paddle spins and a mysterious whirring noise is produced. All over the world the bull-roarer is a real noise-maker.

The Apache people are the only Indians who have a stringed instrument of any kind. It is known as an Apache fiddle and has only one string and a bow. This tribe saw the fiddle of their neighbors, the Mexicans, and adapted it to their own use.

With these comparatively simple musical instruments the American Indians perform their many songs and ceremonials. In later pages of this book the importance of these instruments is discussed in connection with certain ceremonies. All that are mentioned can be heard in the recording, and specimens can be seen in many museums.

SONG-POETRY IN INDIAN MUSIC

■   There is a strong link between music and poetry in the life of the Indian people. They have shown great imagination in the creation of the poetry which is found in the words of their songs. These words usually are based on experiences the Indians feel and know.

Many songs use but few words. The ideas in these songs are very brief and completely to the point. Some of the songs contain words interpreting nature and many of them are filled with great beauty and charm. When you listen to many Indian songs you will hear also meaningless sounds like *hi ya ya ya* or *ho ho se ho*. These syllables are used to fill out the remainder of the rhythm of the song just as you have sung *tra la la* or *fa la la* in songs that you know.

This poetry, so brief, expresses a central idea, which is a definite focal point for the song or the ceremony. The words often are mere cues for a whole series of ideas or associations which, in the mind of the Indian, reveal the complete picture related to the purpose of the song. As an example, a song from the Southwest Pueblo of Acoma in New Mexico contained only two words. The song concerned the wish and the need for food, which for the Acomas was corn. The two words were those for "cloud" and "green corn." These cue words were the clue to the complete story in the mind of the Indians who sang and heard them. The words used in certain other ceremonies are given later in this book so that you may better understand the true meaning of the ceremonials. You will discover that certain tribes (the Pueblos of the Southwest, for instance) have lengthy chants that are much like the epic poems found in the literature of many peoples over the world. Other songs might be part of a long cycle used by a medicine man in an elaborate ritual.

Here are some examples of this song-poetry, representing many different Indian tribes. The original languages have been carefully translated into English by those who have made a longtime study of these texts. Some of the poems are based on the *idea* of the song.

ZUNI LULLABY (*New Mexico*)

> *Go to sleep, my little baby,*
> *While I work.*
> *Father will bring in the sheep soon.*
>
> *Go to sleep, my little beetle.*
> *Go to sleep, my little one,*
> *My little jackrabbit.*

DREAM SONG OF A SIOUX (*South Dakota*)

When I was but a child
I dreamed a wondrous dream.
I went upon a mountain;
There I fell asleep.
I heard a voice say,
"Now I will appear to you."
A buffalo said this to me, dreaming.
When I was but a child
I dreamed this wondrous dream.

CHIPPEWA WOMEN'S SONG FOR WAR PARTY (*Minnesota*)

Fare thee well. The time is come
For our sad departing,
We who take the road to war
Travel on a long journey.

Fare thee well. The warrior's eyes
Must not look beside him;
In departing he must see
Only the campfires of the enemy.

Fare thee well. We go to fight
For the tribe's protection,
Yet we know the road to war
Ever is a long journey.

Slowly

In the above song the actual words were translated as "Come, it is time for you to depart. We are going on a long journey." The three verses, paraphrased by Frances Densmore, are given to show the association in the Indian's mind brought about from hearing only the three key words sung by the warriors when departing and by the women who returned to camp alone. A mere word or thought can bring about a complete picture or story.

SIOUX WARRIOR'S SONG TO HIS HORSE (*South Dakota*)

> *My horse be swift in flight*
> *Even like a bird;*
> *My horse be swift in flight.*
> *Bear me now in safety*
> *Far from the enemy's arrows,*
> *And you shall be rewarded*
> *With streamers and ribbons red.*

CHIPPEWA HUNTING SONG (*Minnesota*)

> *Like a star I shine.*
> *The animal, gazing, is fascinated by my light.*
> *My war club resounds through the sky*
> *To summon the animals to my call.*

WINNEBAGO FLAG SONG (*Wisconsin*)

> *Our beloved flag went across the water to help us fight.*
> *Are you really glad to see*
> *it back again?*

The Winnebago flag, a long, feathered staff, is symbolic of the history and brave deeds of the tribe. This song, with its expressive text, was sung by victorious warriors when they returned to their own people. It shows the respect and symbolic significance of an emblem which was displayed on this occasion with the Stars and Stripes of America.

Later in this book you will read other song-poems related to specific ceremonials.

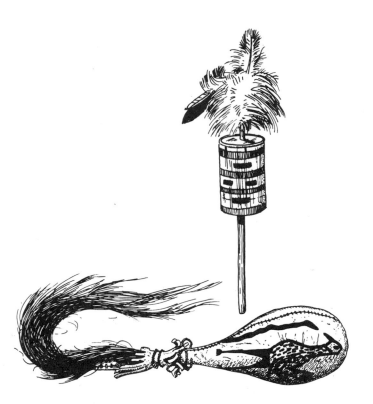

THE DANCE IN INDIAN LIFE

■ Dancing and song were for the Indian people the very heart and soul of life. The dance represented another contact with nature, with all living things. When he danced the Indian came in closer contact with the complete universe which for him included all life. This expression of the dance, combined with song and ritual, completed his world and improved his relationship with things seen and unseen.

An old Indian said, "Dance is part of our religious experience, what some call worship. Some people go to church. We go to a dance."

Associated with the serious affairs of life, dancing was for the Indians connected with processions and observances, with their agriculture and the hunting season, with war and with magic.

Many of the dances once performed by Indians no longer exist. They have been forgotten because they are no longer useful in Indian life. Perhaps they were once part of a ceremony that is no longer performed. Many significant ceremonies were suppressed because the white people believed that the Indians were always "war dancing," and that if they stopped such things it would help destroy the Indians, perhaps crush their spirit. Thus, Indian social, political, and even religious life would pass away. When these things, so important to Indian life, were forbidden, the Indians did lose a significant part of their

lives. The organization of the tribes collapsed. The Indians were indeed crushed.

In later times (as late as the 1930's), when certain dances and ceremonies suppressed during the nineteenth century were allowed to resume, the Indians found it impossible to continue the old ways. Much of the ritual had been forgotten, many of the songs lost, many of the dances not remembered. It was too late for most of the tribes. During the old days, however, dance was completely interwoven into daily life. Many of the oldest dances were ceremonial in character and were symbolic. Some of them were more pageant than dance.

In his effort to move closer to the source of power in nature, the Indian imitated or tried to become a strong part of the natural world around him. Just as he received power through his songs, the Indian knew that in dance he could contact the unseen or the unknown which would give him power. Thus, his dances often imitated birds and animals or spirits that might benefit him when he needed them. His body moved like the deer, the buffalo, the eagle, or even the Thunderbird, and in turn the Indian knew that powerful spirits would aid him and his people. This was another method of appeal to spiritual forces and a means of communication with them. The Indian felt he placed himself in harmony with the natural world around him, and through song and dance made contact with the

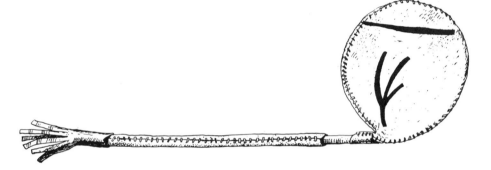

controlling powers in the universe.

Most of the ceremonies involved dancing. There were dances for war, for peace, for joy, for sorrow. Other dances were petitions for rain, for good hunting, good fishing, or anything else the Indian needed in his life.

These dances were not actually complicated. There was a set pattern for most of them. Many of them connected with ritual were rehearsed and perfected before the ceremonies began. True, many of the dances were strenuous, but there was much more involved than hopping, jumping, or leaping. Indian dancers were as graceful as the deer they imitated. They could give the impression of the soaring eagle or the heavy-footed buffalo. The dances were usually performed in the same manner year after year.

Dance patterns are definite, and these forms are traditional and conventional. The steps are executed with great simplicity which proves the skill and grace of the dancers. Most of the dances seem relaxed, perfectly controlled, and very dignified, even though some are extremely vigorous. They are never frenzied. Dance movements are associated with whatever the Indian is seeking to accomplish. Many times the dancers interpret stories and events. In the Buffalo Dance, for example, movements of the large animal are imitated by the performers who mime the hunt, wearing headdresses and robes made

from the animal itself.

There are certain obvious characteristics in Indian dancing. A bent-knee position is often seen. The dancers' back is usually perfectly straight, the body in an erect position. There is much head movement, many times suggestive of the birds and animals in their natural motion. The arms are seldom used except when the dancer represents the soaring eagle or the Thunderbird.

Some of the dances are even simpler. Nowadays many tribes perform the so-called Squaw Dance, including both men and women. It is based on an old-type dance originally connected with some important phase of Indian life which no longer exists. The dance consists merely of a circle of dancers who shuffle their feet alternately as they move to the left. Each man in the circle stands between two women with his right arm around his partner's waist or shoulder. This is similar to the two-step dance, sometimes called Friendship Dance. Other dances include only rising and falling on the toes without moving positions. In certain war dances the men, brisk and vigorous, stamp the ground with their feet and pantomime martial exploits.

Several types of dances are described in the pages devoted to ceremonies and their functions. Diagrams and instructions for four typical dances are shown at the end of this chapter.

Indian life was filled with ritual and ceremony and there was great drama in all these activities. These functions are filled with colorful pageantry. Gods and heroes are represented in brilliant costumes along with the representations of animals and animal spirits, as well as supernatural beings. Masks and costumes transform the Indians into greater beings, and they dance and march in their ceremonies to appeal to those things that go above and beyond human power.

Dancing is for most of us merely a form of amusement and exercise. The Indians dance for pleasure also and for them it is a true social function. But dance is also a sacred thing for the Indian who uses it to charge his atmosphere with much that he could not hope to gain if he lost contact with the complete universe.

■ There are many types of dance steps among the Indians. Here are some of the best-known ones that may be easy for you to learn.

THE TOE-HEEL STEP: Simplest and best-known Indian dance, this takes practice to develop the proper rhythm, which is set by the drumbeat, a ONE-two beat, LOUD-soft. On the *loud* beat of the drum, touch the ground lightly with the left toe (Position 1). Then bring the left heel down hard on the *soft* beat of the drum (Position 2). Repeat with the right foot. Alternate left and right feet, and after you feel comfortable doing this, try variations. Go forward with your group in a circle, go backward, or from side to side.

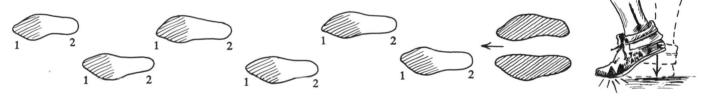

THE DRAG STEP: The drum beats one-TWO, as in the Toe-Heel Dance, but here the soft beat comes first. Step forward on the *soft* first beat so that your toe touches the ground. Then drag the foot backward, letting the heel down hard on the *loud* second beat. Do it lightly or you will wear out your moccasins. This usually is a solo dance.

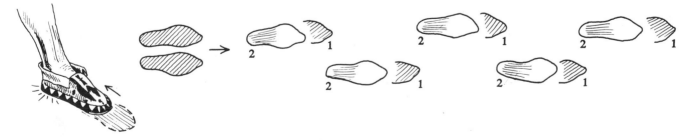

THE STOMP STEP: This dance takes more energy. Body upright with hands close to body at hip height. The drum beats ONE-two-three. On Beat ONE (*loud*) lift knee high and bring foot down hard to ground with stomping motion. On Beats two-three (light beats of drum) come down in two hops on toes. Try this with turtle shell or other rattles tied just below the knees and with rattle in your right hand. Your right forearm should move up and down in time with right foot, the left arm always being inactive. This step is seen in many Pueblo dances in the Southwest.

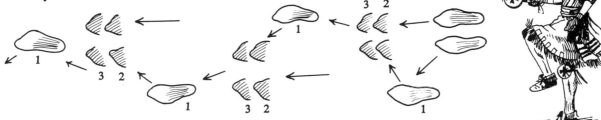

THE CANOE STEP: The drum beats ONE-two-three-four. Swing your arms and body in movements which imitate those of rowing a canoe — long swinging strokes, as if holding a canoe paddle, first on one side of the body, then on the other. On Beat ONE step on your left foot and tap the right foot (as in diagram) on *two-three-four,* stepping forward on the right foot on *ONE*. Then tap the left foot on the next *two-three-four* and step forward on the left foot on *ONE*. After you have mastered this, make a short, quick jump forward on *ONE* instead of just stepping forward on one foot.

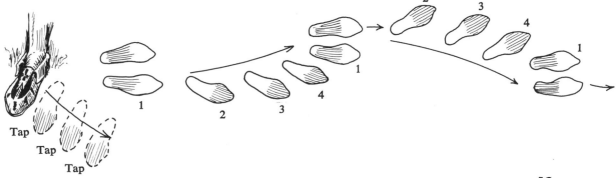

SPIRITS, GODS, MYTHS, AND MYSTERIES IN RITUAL AND CEREMONY

■ We have read in this book about the Indian's belief in certain powerful spirits, of his strong feeling for nature, and of his belief that all living things have power. For the Indian there were certain gods and spirits that were close to him personally and there were other beings that helped the entire tribe and contributed to its welfare.

The ceremonies that the Indians performed at various times of the year were closely associated with these beings, this kind of thinking, and the need to "go beyond human power." Some of this was done through the work of the medicine men who had personal songs, as well as through the songs of other individuals. Throughout the tribe there were always medicine doctors, priests, and others of high rank. Specially selected individuals who had gained high rank or honor among the people participated in ritual. Among the tribes were sacred societies, a variety of clans, and fraternities.

Each tribe had its special ceremonies even though many tribes had variations on some of the same ideas. Many Plains tribes had their own version of the Sun Dance just as many Southwest Pueblo tribes varied their ritual to promote rainfall or to make the corn grow. In other parts of the country one finds rituals for the hunters or the food gatherers. Most of the ceremonies generally referred in some manner to the food supply.

So the ceremonies vary according to the needs of the tribe. Most tribes have certain

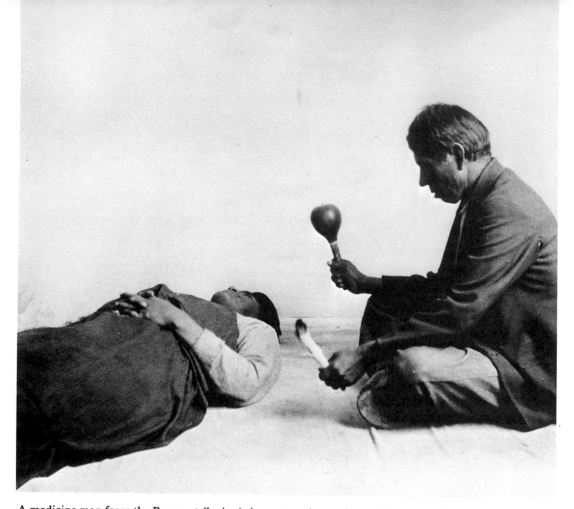

A medicine man from the Papago tribe in Arizona, treating patient with songs, using rattle and deer tail.

acts, such as those connected with naming a child or the ritual of preparing certain medicines. These are done by individuals or by a few people and do not compare with the more elaborate, dramatic ceremonies in which much of the tribe participates. An expression of deep feeling is connected with all true ceremonies held for the renewal and continuance of the tribe, thus strengthening the entire community.

Such ceremonies usually have two parts — the greater and lengthier part which is secret, the last part for the public. There is a priest who serves as leader and advisor. A ceremonial altar, which contains ceremonial articles, such as a sacred bundle, usually is built. As in many religious services, there are a set ritual that is recited, certain songs that are always sung, and dances or pantomimes that show the purpose or tell the story involved with the ceremony. Many of the movements, acts of motion, or marching and dancing, appear very repetitious and simple. But one must remember that each movement is symbolic and has a specific, definite, and important reason.

A stately procession of priests usually begins the public part of a ceremony. There are speeches, recited rituals, and songs, all given in accordance with the purpose of the ceremony. Some ceremonies last for many days; some recited rituals require several hours.

On the following pages certain important ceremonies will be introduced and explained. The importance of these ceremonies in Indian life will be stressed and explanations as to *how* and *why* they were given will be presented.

■ The Indian people believed that a man could not succeed without power. We have learned that much of his power came through certain songs and that these songs when properly used were of great benefit to the singer and to all the tribe. Many times the songs were given to some individual through a dream or vision while he was fasting.

The Great Mystery, sometimes called Great Spirit, was the all-powerful being for many of the Plains Indians. The Sioux called this being *Wakan Tanka*. These two words actually mean "mysterious" and "great." The word *wakan* also applies to a sacred or powerful object or person. Thus, an Indian would say, "This is *wakan*," or "He is *wakan*." A pipe would be something *wakan* because with it prayers and supplications could be made. From this *wakan* object good could be obtained. Such objects became sacred because they were associated also with the Great Mystery, *Wakan Tanka*. All tribes had names for this power. The Omaha called it *Wakonda;* the Pawnee name was *Kawaharu*. The Iroquois word *orenda* is associated with a universal indwelling spirit.

A person who was pure in body and spirit could receive the *wakan* power. This could be done after much fasting and meditation. Throughout his life an Indian could fast and meditate to commune with powers or try to contact such powers that would help him and his people. The old Indians called this "crying for a vision." A young boy, just before manhood, could achieve this if he followed the rules. Usually the boy went to some secluded spot, fasted, and after days without water or food received some kind of message. A buffalo or eagle, bear, or some other bird or animal would appear, sing songs, give instructions to the young brave. The supernatural being, in a certain form, would guide the Indian as to the use of the power given him.

An old Indian father said, "You should try to be of some benefit to your fellowmen, my son. If you do not obtain a spirit to strengthen you, you will amount to nothing in the estimation of your fellowmen. Be sure to make yourself the possessor of superhuman power by the aid of the animal that you have seen in your vision after fasting."

The Plains Indians begin to prepare themselves for a vision by first seeking the solitude of nature. They go to a place undisturbed by man. With fasting and meditation, they think of what the vision might be. The vision-seeker loses himself within the forces of nature and when what he seeks comes to him he takes it with thanks and makes it his own.

A young Sioux warrior dreamed that he would be aided throughout his life by the owl and the crow. Here is his personal medicine song.

At night may I roam,
Against the winds may I roam,
At night may I roam,
When the owl is hooting may I roam.

At dawn may I roam,
Against the winds may I roam,
At dawn may I roam,
When the crow is calling may I roam.

A medicine man received in a vision this song, which was sung to him in a lodge filled with buffalo and gave him the power to practice his medicine.

"I will appear.
Behold me!"
A buffalo said to me.

Several other songs received in visions are given in the chapter related to song-poetry and in the pages devoted to the medicine men.

MEDICINE POWER THROUGH SONG

■ Indian doctors—medicine men—held a high position in their tribes and were considered as or sometimes more important than the chief or the leading warriors. These men, and women, could do all manner of things. Many of them not only could cure diseases, but seemed to have supernatural power to predict future events. They could tell the best time for a hunting or war party. Thus, they were both healers and seers.

Many of these doctors gained knowledge from visions and dreams. A powerful spirit might have told them how to heal ailments, advising which plants, herbs, roots, to use for certain illnesses. And, as we read in an earlier chapter, the songs given to the medicine man by a dream spirit, combined with the use of drugs, completed a personal or public medicine rite. There were at least two methods of treating the sick among Indians—a private as well as a public one.

In a public ceremony many doctors participate; the rite is attended by many people and is continued for several days. These doctors are regarded with great respect and it is reported that they are usually quiet, dignified men who live strictly in accordance with

the requirements of their dreams. Sometimes a medicine man is assisted by his wife, usually his only companion. He lives in quiet seclusion and seems to be aware of the forces of nature, its power, and its benefits for himself and for his people.

Some of the great poetry of the Indian people is found in the words of medicine songs. You will find examples in this book as well as descriptions of ceremonies in which medicine men play a leading part.

The Chippewa Indians of Minnesota have a well-organized Grand Medicine Society known as the *Mide-wiwin*. Many members associated with it go through at least four initiations to reach high office. The emblem of the Society is a small cowrielike shell known as *migis*. This shell has great medicinal use and has magical significance. The *Mide*, or Grand Medicine, is the native religion of the Chippewa. It teaches that goodness makes for a long life and that evil eventually destroys the offender. The medicine men play a great part in ensuring health and long life, which is the purpose of the Society. There are many songs used in the *Mide-wiwin* ceremonies that fulfill this purpose. The ritual contains sacred formulas being handed down; its origin is in dream revelations.

Many of the songs of the *Mide-wiwin* refer in part to the sacred symbols, especially the shell, or perhaps animal spirits involved with the rituals.

My life, my single tree — we dance around you.
All around the circle of the sky I hear the
*   Spirit's voice.*

I walk upon half of the sky.
I am the crow, his skin is in my body.

Navaho medicine men and priests hold healing rites and exorcise evil spirits from the sick with songs and rattles. Many of these chanters wear masks.

The herb-gathering songs are heard when the plant is to be cooked for good medicine. It is not the herb that fights against the disease but the "spirit" of the herb that fights against the "spirit" of the disease.

> *The Spirit placed medicine in the ground;*
> *Let us take it.*
> *I have the medicine in my heart.*
> *Yes, there is much medicine you may cry for.*
> *I am as strong as the bear.*
>
> *This is for a good purpose.*
> *It will be successful.*

The power of the Society, its songs and its rituals, are all felt, as shown in the following.

> *Verily the sky clears when my Mide drum*
> *sounds for me.*
> *Verily the waters are smooth when my Mide drum*
> *sounds for me.*
>
> *There comes a sound from my medicine bag.*
> *You will recover, you will walk again.*
> *It is I who say it.*
>
> *My power is great.*
> *Through our white shell I will enable*
> *you to walk again.*
>
> *This is for a good purpose.*
> *It will be successful.*

The words of the following song refer to the dream in which the doctor received his power, dreaming of the mighty Thunderbird, who gave instructions for this healing song.

> *Hear the loud sound!*
> *The Thunderbirds draw near us, in their*
>   *mighty power.*
> *Hear their voices!*
> *The lightning flash is the gleaming of*
>   *their terrible eyes;*
> *The roll in the storm-swept sky*
> *Is the noise of the Thunderbirds' wings.*

Drum

The ancient teachings and beliefs of the *Mide* are preserved in the words of their many songs. The Indians never wrote down their music or even the words of their songs in any notation. However, the Chippewa used strips of birchbark to preserve their songs and ceremony in a type of picture writing called mnemonics. These pictures serve as a reminder of the idea of the songs, not an actual notation of notes or words as in our musical scores. Every member of the *Mide-wiwin* understands these drawings and knows the songs they represent.

A pictographic song record is shown in a photograph from the Chippewa Grand Medicine Society. The signs and symbols are typical and show circles and string or wavy

lines. The circle is used to represent the earth or the sky and sometimes a lake or a hill. The other lines are connected to "spirit power." Other symbolic drawings represent objects or beings connected with tribal life or things involved in the ceremony.

Thus, the power of the *Mide* is exerted through a combination of two mediums, music and medicine. The healing power of music combined with other aspects of ritual and ceremony is part of the life of many primitive peoples over the world. It sustains and strengthens the life of the tribes, and all the people honor and respect their tribal doctor, who is indeed a real "musical therapist."

THE SACRED PIPE OF THE OGLALA SIOUX

■   It is long ago that the White Buffalo Maiden appeared on the Plains and brought the Sacred Pipe and the knowledge of it. She first appeared before two young men who were hunting buffalo and when they saw this beautiful woman dressed in the most lovely clothes they were amazed. The Maiden spoke to them and said, "I am of the Buffalo People and I have been sent to this earth to talk with your people. Take me to your people so that I may bring them some important messages and knowledge."

This mysterious visitor, this *wakan* woman from the Buffalo People, appeared at the camp of the Oglala Sioux and was welcomed as a sister in great honor. When she spoke to all the people she said, "Because you have been reverent and faithful, because you have preserved good against evil and harmony against discord, you have been chosen to receive the pipe which I now hold, in behalf of all mankind. This pipe is a symbol of peace and should be used as such between men and nations. Smoking the pipe is a bond of good faith and some of you can be in communion with the *Wakan Tanka*, the Great Mystery."

The White Buffalo Maiden explained to the people how to care for the pipe, how to use it, how to offer sacrifices and prayers to the *Wakan Tanka* for the blessings of life. "Through this pipe your nation lives," she explained. "As a sacred instrument of preservation it should be used in times of war, famine, sickness, or any other need." Then she revealed to them the seven sacred rituals, ceremonies they were to practice:

Purification (the sweat lodge),

Seeking of the Vision (dream power),

The Sun Dance (renewal of strength),

The Rite of Relationship (with men and with the *Wakan Tanka*),

Preparing a Girl for Womanhood,

Ball Throwing (sacred game),

Soul Keeping (purifying the souls of the dead).

After she had spoken and after she had given her message and instruction, the White Buffalo Maiden offered the Sacred Pipe and smoked it with the people. Then she announced that her mission was finished, and laying the pipe against the rack, she left the village unescorted. While everyone watched her disappear, she was transformed into a white buffalo calf. This daughter of the Sun and Moon had brought her message to earth and people still speak of her as The Beautiful One.

The Sacred Pipe is continually used in ceremonies by the Oglala Sioux and other Plains Indians. The Indians named the pipe the White Buffalo Calf Pipe. Duplicates of it were made, and soon every man of the tribe carried a similar pipe.

The following song was said to have been sung by the White Buffalo Maiden as she entered the camp.

With visible breath
I am walking toward the Buffalo nation.
My voice is heard.
I am walking with visible breath.

The "visible breath" indicates the breath of the buffalo rising in the frosty air in cold weather.

Smoke-offering to the Great Mystery is a widespread ceremony among the American Indians. The pipe is symbolic and tobacco is sacred. The purifying, life-giving power of such things as smoke, fire, ashes, is sacred to these people. Rising smoke may carry messages to the Creator. This smoke represents the breath of life. Thus, the Sacred Pipe is the symbol of the tribe and keeps it united through its songs and ceremonies.

THE SUN DANCE OF THE PLAINS

Wakan-Tanka, have mercy on us,
That our people may live!

■ So sang the Oglala Sioux of the Plains. This was a song from one of the great sacred rites of these Indian people — the Dance Looking at the Sun, or in their language, the *wiwanyag wachipi*. Many people called it the Sun Dance but that is not its true name. The ceremony came to the Sioux and other Plains tribes many years after the coming of the White Buffalo Maiden.

This ceremony is held in June or July during the time of the full moon. At this time the Indians say that "the eternal light of the Great Mystery is upon the whole world." It is at the time of the summer buffalo hunt when all of the people gather together, and for a week or more there are many minor ceremonies climaxed with the Sun Gazing Dance.

A man usually initiates the ceremony because it is necessary for him to fulfill a vow which he had made at a time of great distress. Perhaps he had asked for success in war,

or had asked that his wife or brother be cured of sickness. If successful, this man would make a sacrifice at the ceremony to complete his promise. Others could join him, and the whole life and strength of the tribe was renewed. The idea is one of thanksgiving and provides another chance to ask for supernatural power and strength.

Some tribes call this ceremony the Torture Dance. Some gashes are cut in the breast and a cord of sinew, or a skewer, is tied through the gashes. The long cord is fastened to a pole — the Sun Dance pole in the center of the Sun Dance Lodge. The pledgers, to fulfill their vows, dance in supplication for supernatural powers, denying themselves both food and drink. They steadily gaze at the sun or at the offerings on the sacred pole. Sacred objects hang on the sacred pole — a bundle of brush, a buffalo hide or buffalo skull, cloth, and other offerings. The skewers or thongs fastened to the men's breasts or backs pull out and tear out as they dance. If the men fall unconscious from pain this is their moment of contact with the supernatural. Many of the men blow bone whistles

while they rise and fall on their toes. Some claim this keeps them from crying out in pain.

This Torture Dance, which was indeed self-infliction, even though it was one of the great religious ceremonies of these people, was forbidden by the government many years ago. As recently as 1940, it was resumed and can be seen today among many Plains tribes. This photograph was made in the summer of 1965.

The words of a song included in this ceremony are:

> *They say a herd of buffalo is coming.*
> *It is here now!*
> *Their blessing will come to us.*
> *It is with us now!*
>
> *The Sun, the Light of the world,*
> *I hear Him coming!*
> *I see His face as He comes.*
> *He makes the beings on earth happy,*
> *And they rejoice.*
> *O Wakan-Tanka, I offer You*
>   *this world of Light!*
> *This sacred day You made the buffalo roam.*
> *You have made a happy day for the world.*
> *I offer all to You!*

The men attached to the sacred pole have special songs:

Wakan-Tanka, be merciful to me.
We want to live!
That is why we are doing this.

In this ceremony the drum plays an important part and except for the whistle is the only instrument used. An old Indian said, "Because the drum is round it represents the whole universe, and its steady strong beat is the pulse, the heart, throbbing at the center of the universe. It is as the voice of Wakan-Tanka and this sound stirs us and helps us to understand the mystery and power of all things."

When this great and sacred ritual of the Plains was taken away from these people the Indians felt that all was lost. Today, in our own time, they have renewed their faith with the past, and the power brought to them through years of renewal still lives and is remembered. One can now see the Sun Dance revived on the reservations and the brave ones once again sing

Wakan-Tanka, be merciful to us!
We want to live!
That is why we are doing this.

■ Corn, or maize, was the most important food among most Indian tribes. Because of its significance for the life of the tribes it is natural that there would be a great many ceremonies and rites connected with it. Many of these ceremonies are related to the planting, growing, and harvesting of the corn. Many of them are an important part of a thanksgiving rite.

The tribes of the eastern woodlands held what was called the Green Corn Dance and it was a ceremony of thanksgiving. With the first ripening of corn in summer many of these tribes in the southern part of the country celebrated what was to them the new year. The rites took eight days, and this was also a time to clear all obligations and debts, and was a time for forgiveness. Many things were involved in this complex ritual. First, it meant cleaning the town or village, extinguishing all fires, and lighting new ones. The

men drank a special liquid that cleansed and purified them. Then they fasted before the new corn was tasted for the first time. There were many songs and dances during this time. Ceremonial games were played.

The photograph of the small diorama from an exhibit at the American Museum of Natural History shows part of the Green Corn Dance as it was performed over a century ago among the Creeks and Cherokees. In a public square of the town, four sacred logs are brought by four young men, while four other young men approach carrying ears of new corn that priests will place on the fire. No women or children are allowed at this part of the ceremony even though they may participate in all the other rites during the eight days. Men are seated according to their clan affiliation and office. The priest lights the new fire, celebrating the new year, blessing the corn, and giving thanks. These significant rituals are part of the ceremonial life of the Creeks, Cherokees, Seminoles, and others of the southern woodlands. Some of the tribes also use these eight days for curing diseases, and combating illnesses. It is a time for renewing the strength and well-being of the Indian people.

Green Corn Festivals are also held among the Iroquois, but in early September. There are various rites of thanksgiving—the Great Feather Dance and many social dances, as well as ceremonies for the corn itself. The songs are addressed to the spirit of the corn, said to be the most important of the three life-sustaining sisters — corn, beans, and squash. These are the food spirits, and are honored in several songs and dances.

The Pueblo Indians have elaborate and very beautiful dances concerning the corn, dances for the crops, the rain cloud, the harvest. Yellow Corn Maidens and Rainbow Maidens are featured in these dances, each group having elaborate headdresses, called *tablites*, and decorative costumes.

Nicely while it is raining,
Corn plant, I am singing for you,
Nicely while the water is streaming,
Vine plant, I am singing for you.

ACOMA PUEBLO *(New Mexico)*

My dears, you yellow corn maidens,
As you rise up I see you,
Then I sing for you.

Come, let us go,
Yellow and blue, as you come to meet one another,
We go right on, we go right up and out
into the open spaces.

COCHITI PUEBLO *(New Mexico)*

THE FALSE FACE SOCIETY OF THE IROQUOIS

■ The men of the Iroquois Society of False Faces carve wooden masks that represent supernatural beings that they believe to be evil spirits. Members of the Society wear these masks in ceremonies concerned with curing diseases, controlling plagues, and driving away evil. The masks represent mythical, bodiless beings that live in the forest, terrifying and grotesque beings that were often seen by woodland Indians.

In the old days the masks were carved from living trees. The carver went to the forest after he had dreamed of what the mask would be; then he selected the tree, which was usually basswood. Sacred tobacco was burned at the base of the tree as an offering. A medicine man rubbed the bark with a turtle shell rattle as he spoke prayers. The medicine man asked the tree to share its life spirit with the mask about to be carved from its trunk. These masks are meant to show weird, ugly, and distorted features because they are worn when frightening away the spirits of evil related to sickness.

To become a member of the False Face Society, a person must have a dream in which a False Face appears, or he must be one who has been cured of an illness by the Society. Women as well as men may become members, but only men wear masks.

Members are summoned by a sick person or his family. They appear as a group, masked and shaking turtle shell rattles, muttering, groaning, and making weird noises. Inside the house the False Faces sprinkle ashes over the sick person and shake their rattles over him. Tobacco again plays a great part in the ritual and the members are rewarded with gifts of food, especially a "False Face mush" made of cornmeal. In the spring and fall the members go from house to house exorcising evil and disease. First a marching song is sung when members enter a dwelling. It is a song that appeals to the wind spirits the masks represent.

"A voice is rising . . . "

Speeches are made and more songs are sung.

"The great good mask has a smiling face . . . "

After this there are the songs of the "Bushy-heads" or Husk Faces, men wearing masks of braided corn husks. These supposedly represent beings who brought garden seeds to the Iroquois in the early days. Although related to agriculture, these members also are able to conduct cures.

The rattles used to beat the tempo of False Face Society songs are made from turtles, rattles from about 10 inches to 1 foot long. These rattles are symbolic of the Iroquois belief that the very earth rests on the back of a snapping-turtle. Often the singer sits on a wooden bench, striking the board with the edge of the turtle shell.

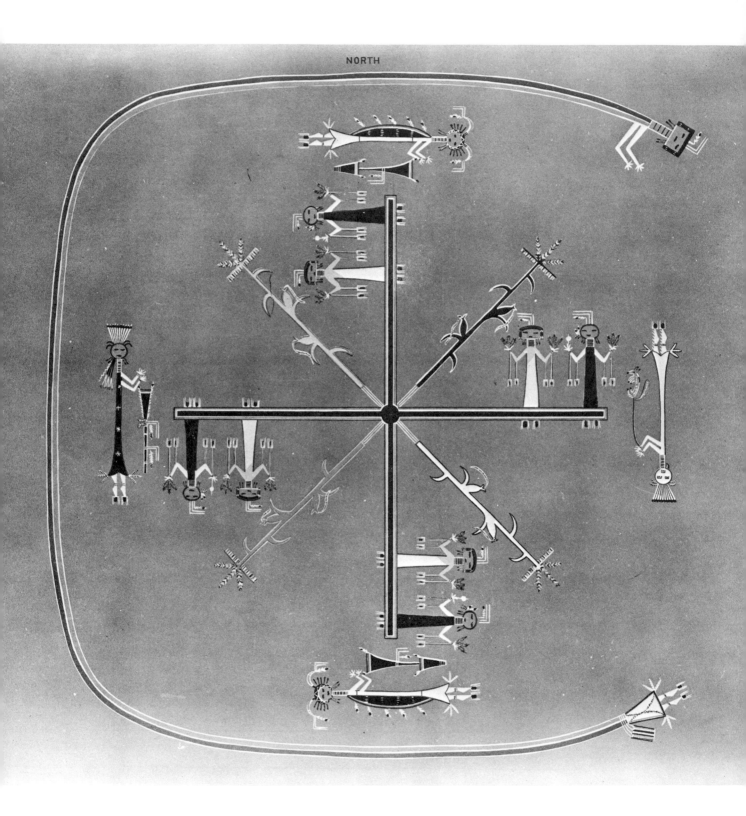

NAVAHO CHANTS AND DRY PAINTINGS

■ The old Indians believe that the gods were the first to make pictures in sand. The Navaho said that the gods made pictures on black clouds spread on the floor. Since this was impossible for the people to do, they used sand instead, and the people said that sand was very good because then no outsiders could steal the paintings.

What was the purpose of these so-called paintings?

These beautiful masterpieces, created only for one single day, have magical and supernatural significance. They are made to be used in a healing rite·and for the purpose of destroying disease or evil. Through these paintings made from dry materials the gods are said to enter the bodies of those seeking a cure. Thus, the power of the painting enters to cleanse and purify the patient.

Colored sand, cornmeal, crushed flowers are used to make the symbolic designs used in these ceremonies. A priest or medicine man begins early in the day to put his design on the floor or ground. With an assistant, he has to complete his work within hours. After the painting is completed the patient sits upon it and the ceremony continues with songs and the application of herbs and medicinal plants. The doctor, who is the artist, summons forth the healing spirits to remove the disease from the sufferer's body.

Many of the Pueblo Indians use dry paintings in healing ceremonies and as decorations for their underground temples, or kivas. The Navaho paintings, however, are the best known and most popular. There are hundreds of different dry paintings for this sacred ritual, depending upon the nature of the illness.

The ceremony itself is generally referred to as a "sing" or a chant or a prayer. The sick person's family calls upon the medicine man who comes to the dwelling, diagnoses the illness, and then decides which prayer or sing should be given. There is a painting for each song and the medicine man has to know all the chants and remember each design for the paintings. Special sand grains, meal, or flowers must be collected and prepared. Green boughs are brought, arranged in an arch through which the sick person

must pass. The color green means fertile crops and fertility means good health. The painting sometimes takes six or more hours to complete and the sick person does not see the painting until it is entirely completed. First, many prayers must be chanted.

All paintings face eastward, the direction of the rising sun, and the patient enters the design from the east. Once the person is seated on the painting the design is disturbed. This means the power has been drawn into the patient to help the curing. With more songs and the anointing with sacred water and a sacred meal the ceremony continues. Smoke from a sacred fire is rubbed onto the body to carry the disease or evil spirit out of the body. The Indians say, "The disease goes up in smoke." The patient is seated for about an hour and then is taken home.

The medicine man now destroys the painting in the reverse order from which he made it. If the painting is not destroyed before sundown, evil spirits of the darkness will be attracted by it and will cause harm.

The lengthy chants of the Navaho medicine man are filled with great and beautiful poetry and poetic thought. With the chants, the dry paintings, and the other elaborate parts of the ritual, the patient's health and well-being are restored and he leaves the ceremony with renewed faith in the future because the power of the gods has entered him and thus given him strength.

I have made your sacrifice.
I have prepared your smoke for you.

My body restore for me.
My mind restore for me.

Impervious to pain, may I walk.
Feeling light within, I walk.
With lively feelings, may I walk.
Happily may I walk.
Happily abundant dark clouds I desire.
Happily abundant showers I desire.
Happily abundant vegetation I desire.
May it be happy before me.
May it be happy behind me.
May it be happy below me.
May it be happy above me.

With it happy all around me, may I walk.
It is finished in beauty.
It is finished in beauty.

THE SNAKE DANCE OF THE HOPI

Behold, brothers!
Behold, men of the snake!
Behold!
The unseen ones have heard our prayers.
Black clouds gather over distant hills.
Behold, brothers!
Behold, men of the snake!

■ This is part of a long cycle of songs that the Hopi Snake Clan members sing in a summer ceremony held to ask for rainfall over their desertland. It is a sensational ceremony for those who witness it because live snakes are handled by the Hopi in their ritual and these snakes are often held in the mouth of the dancers. The ceremony, part of a nine-day ritual, is a very old one and is probably one of the most ancient still in existence today.

Snakes were supposed to be the guardians of springs and were associated with water. Therefore, the snake is a clan ancestor of the Hopi, and is worshipped as such. The ceremony takes place in August at the time when the kachinas return to their mountain home. You will read of the kachinas and their ceremonies in the next part of this chapter.

The Hopi believe that in asking for rainfall, the snakes carry the urgent message directly to the gods. The ceremony is held in the underground kiva, except for the last day. Only members of the clan participate in the sacred ritual. Outsiders can only witness the final day of the ceremony.

In preparation, prayer sticks — ornamented and colorfully made feathered staffs — are placed in holy places, especially near springs. Then the members go out snake hunting. For almost a week snakes are collected and held captive in pottery jars. Priests bring in almost every snake they can capture, even though rattlers are the most desirable. Rituals are held in the kiva and on the final day the snakes are washed and brought to the village to be used for the final dance in the plaza. The snakes are kept in a *kisi* — a small shelter made of cottonwood boughs — and brought out as they are used in the dance. The dancers form a line in groups of three and dance with a hopping step to the *kisi*. There each dancer is handed a snake which he grasps by the middle in his mouth and then dances four times around the plaza. This action is repeated by all of the snake priests. Women and maidens in picturesque costumes, standing on one side of the plaza, sprinkle the dancers with sacred meal from basket trays. When all the snakes have been carried, a "picture" is drawn on the ground with sacred cornmeal and the snakes are thrown on the meal. A wild scramble, and the priests grasp the snakes in their hands and rush away from the village to release the reptiles to the four directions, asking that they take their prayers to the rain gods. Meanwhile black clouds are usually seen gathering over the village and the people know that their prayers have been answered. They know that their clan ancestors, the snakes, have delivered their message. They know, too, that their ceremony has been performed so correctly that the rain gods are pleased. The desert area will now be less dry, corn will grow, and there will be a bountiful harvest for the Hopi who have renewed their age-old tradition in the Snake Ceremony.

KACHINA SPIRITS AND THE DOLLS OF THE HOPI AND ZUNI

■ Many of the Indians of the Pueblo in the Southwest, particularly the Hopi and the Zuni, have a number of ceremonies in which masked characters called kachinas appear. These characters, which are supposed to be supernatural beings, are impersonated by men of the tribes wearing masks. Several hundred different kachinas are said to live in the high mountains, especially the San Francisco Peaks in Arizona. At special times the kachinas leave their mountain homes and come down to the Hopi villages to perform their ceremonials and assist the Pueblo people. These ceremonies involving the kachinas are among the most colorful of all ritual pageants to be seen among the American Indians. If you travel to the Southwest you can still see many of the old dances. The symbolic masks represent some of the most famous kachina characters, from the most serious gods to the clownish mudheads. An old Indian said, "Long ago in old times the kachinas lived upon the earth. They danced before us and brought rain. No more they come. So to bring rain our people become kachinas in dress, mask, and body paint." Thus, the ancient customs continue, are remembered and preserved. Rain again falls on the arid desertland and the corn blossoms forth and brings a bountiful harvest to the people of the Pueblos. Their petitions and prayers are answered. The supernatural and unseen ones are pleased with the songs and dances, and life continues for the Hopi and their neighbors.

The Hopi and the Zuni Indians think of the kachinas in a number of ways:

(1) as supernatural beings;

(2) as masked impersonators, knowing that they are really selected men of the villages who take on the character of certain kachinas and by donning a mask, become that being;

(3) as kachina dolls made to resemble the masked men themselves.

The Hopi calendar of religious ceremonies consists of two parts: the winter solstice from December to the middle of July, and the summer solstice from mid-July until the next December.

Five kachina ceremonies are held during the first half of the year. These major ceremonies last nine days each. They are held underground in the kivas and only the chosen and initiated may attend or witness them. Only certain parts of these may be seen by the public when members go aboveground to the plazas. About thirty kachinas take part in these major ceremonies. The winter solstice rites, beginning in December, are called *Soy-alang-eu* by the Hopi. *Pamuya* follows in January at the time when the sun appears to move north again. *Powamuya,* a Bean Dance, is held in February, and the Water Serpent Ceremony known as *Pololökonto* follows in February or March. When the sun appears to move north in July the final kachina rite, the *Niman Kachina* or the Home Dance, is held. At that time the kachinas return to their mountain home.

One-day ceremonies are held during this first half of the year, also. These regular kachina dances are seen in the village plazas or main square. Sometimes twenty or more dancers wear the same masks. Other times the costumes are mixed and one meets many different characters. The Pueblo people count this as a time of great festivity and everyone comes from neighboring towns and villages to witness the pageantry. Feasts are always prepared on these social days.

During the second half of the Hopi religious year no masked impersonators take part in ceremonies or dances. From August to December there are a number of ceremonies and one of these was described in the preceding section. The Snake and Antelope fraternities perform their rites at this time. Sometimes one may see ceremonies of the Flute Societies. In September and October come the women's society's functions and in November certain tribal initiation rituals are held. The purpose of most of these ceremonies is to promote rainfall.

But what is the purpose of these kachinas? What is their real meaning in the religion of the Pueblo Indians?

When a Hopi wears a special mask with its appropriate costume he believes that he has become another being. He thinks he has lost his own personality and has received the spirit of the kachina that he impersonates. The Hopi believe that through the kachinas prayers can be carried to the gods.

What are their prayers and what do the Hopi petition in their ceremonies? Rain, good corn crops, and a bountiful harvest are of prime importance to these people living in the semidesert of the Southwest. For centuries they have been faced with a water shortage and have had great difficulties making their land yield enough food.

The Hopi believe that by their songs and prayers the kachinas through supernatural power aid them in the production of food. Each kachina group has characteristic songs. The men of the villages take great care and pride in their masks, body paint, and costumes. They rehearse and memorize the many songs and the dance until the performance is perfect. As the great necessity of the Hopi ceremonial is aid in the production of rain to water their arid farms, the kachinas are called Rain Gods and their songs the Rain and Growth Songs. Some of these songs have been collected and can be heard in a recording.

During the first months of the year the men of the village carve small wooden figures that represent many of the kachinas. These dolls are carved and painted to resemble the masked kachina dancers that appear in the ceremonials. The dolls are not toys even though every girl and boy receives one or more as a gift from the kachinas themselves. They are objects for study to be treasured. By having these figures — called by the Hopi, *tihü* — the children can become familiar with the real kachinas in the ceremonies. Thus, the gift serves as part of religious training, as part of the education of the child.

During the months of December to July the children enjoy many delights and treats. When the kachinas come to earth in February each child expects one of these *tihü*

as a gift. Boys also receive miniature bows and arrows. The children believe these things are made by the kachinas themselves. In addition, they receive fruits, special sweets, and other foods. It would be like our having Christmas every day! If the child has been naughty, the presents are withheld for a time and a kachina pretends to beat the child with a small whip.

In one of the kachina dances masked men dance in single file as they walk quickly into the plaza, forming a line on one side. One verse of a song is heard as the men keep time with their feet. They have rattles in their hands and rattles made from tortoise shells fastened to their legs. Then the line moves to another side of the plaza, then to the next side. Each time the men sing another verse of the song. After the song has been heard at the four directions, the kachinas leave as they distribute presents to the children. In less than an hour they return and repeat the same performance, which can continue to be repeated from noon until about sunset. Six to eight verses of the song will be heard.

In the west at Flower Mountain
A rain priest sits
His head feathered with cumulus clouds.
His words are of clouding over Itawana.
"Come let us arise now."
Thus along the shores of the encircling ocean
The rain makers say to one another.
Aha ehe, aha ehe!

In the south at South Lake Mountain
A rain priest sits
His head feathered with mist.
His words are of covering Itawana with rain.
"Come let us go."
Thus in all the springs
The rain makers say to one another.
Aha ehe, aha ehe!

"The beautiful world germinates.
The sun, the yellow dawn, germinate."
Thus the corn plants say to one another.
They are covered with dew.
They bring forth their young.
Aha ehe, aha ehe!

In this song from the Zuni Pueblo in New Mexico, one hears the rain priests petitioning for rain. The Zuni kachinas are supernatural beings and are associated with the dead — in other words, ancestral spirits of former Zuni people. They are at the same time associated with clouds and rain. The Zuni say these beings live in a nearby lake and come from there when they visit the Zuni villages. These kachinas help to fertilize the earth and to call forth the much-needed rain. The word *Itawana* means the place of the dead.

A corn planting ritual song sung by Hopi kachinas tells of yellow butterflies over the bean blossoms. This is a good example of poetic imagination found in Indian poetry.

Yellow butterflies,
Over the blossoming virgin corn,
With pollen-painted faces
Chase one another in brilliant throng.

Blue butterflies,
Over the blossoming virgin beans,
With pollen-painted faces
Chase one another in brilliant streams.

Over the blossoming corn,
Over the virgin corn,
Wild bees hum;
Over the blossoming beans,
Over the virgin beans,
Wild bees hum.

Over your field of growing corn
All day shall hang the thundercloud;
Over your field of growing corn
All day shall come the rushing rain.

THE DEER DANCE OF THE YAQUI

■ The Yaqui Indians once lived entirely on the Yaqui River in Sonora, northern Mexico. They were said to be a very powerful tribe. When invaders came, the Yaqui would not submit to the political domination of the Mexican government. Many of the Indians left Mexico and crossed into southern Arizona. Today one can find fewer than 3,000 Yaqui in the Southwest but there are many thousands still residing in Mexico. Their culture is very primitive and they have clung to their ancient customs and ceremonies. However, in the seventeenth and eighteenth centuries many of the Yaqui took up Christian practices but did not sacrifice their old ways. Therefore, one finds a mixture of two types of culture and one can see Christian symbols and religious objects used with the ancient primitive dances and pantomimes. During Holy Week there are many festivities which feature masked dancers and Yaqui in ceremonial costumes old and new. The deer and the coyote are popular in the pantomimes.

Once, generations ago, the Yaqui Indians in southern Arizona had a magical ceremony that was said to charm the deer and ensure a successful hunt. The Yaqui brought this ceremony with them from Mexico. This Deer Dance is now the most important event during the spring celebrations, especially during the days around the Christian Eastertime. It is no longer connected with deer hunting.

The Deer Dance is a pantomime which shows the hunt and death of the deer. As *el Venado* roams we can see all the movements of the animal as he sniffs, looks about, hesitates, perhaps scents danger, or drinks water. Masked dancers represent the coyotes. The deer is discovered and the coyotes pursue him. Finally they kill him.

The important dancer in these festivities is *el Venado* — the Deer. On his head the dancer wears a stuffed head of a deer decorated with flowers and ribbons. He wears nothing above his waist. A sash hangs down to his knees. This is held on by a belt which has many deer hoofs attached to it. The dancer's ankles are wrapped in dried butterfly cocoons filled with small pebbles that click together while he dances. In each hand the Deer Dancer carries a large gourd rattle.

At least three musicians accompany the Deer Dancer. The singer, who plays a rasp, is in the center. He has to use a loud voice to be heard above the instruments which are so dynamic that he appears to be merely humming. Another player plays a second rasp, and the third plays a water drum. The water drum is a half-gourd which is turned upside down and floated in a large pan of water. This makes its peculiar sound and serves as resonator. The gourd is steadied as the drummer touches it lightly with the fingers of his left hand. He holds a stick in his right hand, which he calls the "water hitter."

The scraped rasp has three separate parts: the rasping device itself, the rubbing stick, and the resonating gourd. The rasping device itself is a narrow stick made of hard wood

that has many notches across its entire length, which look like small teeth set close together. A smaller stick is rubbed across the notched stick. A half-gourd is placed on the ground upside down and the large stick is placed on the gourd lightly by the player who keeps it from slipping off when the notches are rubbed by the small stick.

The songs are very ancient and indeed very poetic. Here is a free English translation of some of the songs.

> *The mountain grass*
> *Moved with the gently blowing breeze*
> *And whistled softly.*
> *The grass grows on the mountain top*
> *And blows with the wind.*
>
> *The wind is moving the yellow flowers.*
> *The deer looks at a flower.*
>
> *In summer the rains come*
> *And the grass comes up.*
> *That is the time*
> *That the deer has new horns.*
>
> *Deer, deer, deer,*
> *Coyote is hunting you.*
> *Place yourself in the water,*
> *No harm will he do to you.*

When the Deer Dance is performed at other times, such as at a dance program on the stage or at other festivities for the public, several dancers impersonate hunters with bows and arrows who finally kill the deer after stalking it. The Deer Dance is taken out of the primitive setting of ancient days when it was used to charm the deer and ensure a successful hunt for the Yaqui people. A dramatic presentation of the Deer Dance was a highlight in the performances of a dance group which toured the world — the Ballet Folklorico de Mexico. Thus, an old ceremony was adapted to today's needs.

You will hear part of the music for the Deer Dance in the recording with this book. Hear the drum begin the rhythm, followed by *morache* — scraping sticks — and the singer who uses a strange, closed voice that sounds almost like a low-pitched hum.

Drum

Scrapping sticks

SHAMAN AND POTLACH IN THE NORTHWEST

■ Totem poles are the trademark of the Pacific Northwest and the Indians who live there are surrounded by dark, rugged forests of giant red cedar trees and towering sequoia. The totems are a symbol of the area which extends from northern California up into Canada to Alaska, and the Indians are known as Nootka, Quilliute, Coast Salish, Kwakiutl, Bella Coola, Tsimsyan, Haida, and Tlingit. Each of these nations has a great many divisions or tribes. Divisions of the Nootkan peoples — Makah, Neah Bay, Cape Flattery, Quileute, and others — are found in Puget Sound area near Washington State.

These Indians make totem poles from the giant trees and the poles are symbols or identifications of a clan or family. They are not idols to be worshipped. They are like crests or insignia, erected in memory of ancestors and departed chiefs. Some are found as graves, or at gravesites, others are set up in front of houses to identify the inhabitants. The carvings interpret both humans and animals. It is not unusual to see the eagle, the raven, or the whale carved in wood. History and legend of the family are shown, and the pole serves as a sort of coat-of-arms.

Other than totem poles, these Indians along the coast also carve fantastic and unique masks representing many of the same creatures as well as supernatural beings and objects of the natural world, such as the sun and moon. Wooden rattles, showing figures of the Thunderbird, the bear, the wolf, or the raven, are used by medicine men in ceremonies. The masks are worn by dancers or the medicine men — known as shamans — in elaborate ceremonies.

Cedar logs are made into dugout canoes up to 60 feet long by these coastal tribes. All the men live by the sea, and their large boats are worthy of traveling in the ocean and in the coastal waters for fishing and whaling. There are many canoe songs among the tribes, songs sung in paddling motion. The true maritime people were the Makah, the Quinault, and the Quileute. They have songs to calm the sea in rough weather. Many have been preserved and can be heard in recording.

Many of the songs of the Northwest Coast Indians were closely connected with "spirit power" and were said to have been received in dreams and visions. Especially important were songs to promote good fishing. Certain creatures of the sea were held to be guardian spirits. The "killer whale" spirit was held in great awe.

The greatest gift a spirit could give was the power to heal diseases or cure illnesses. A man with such gifts was known as a shaman and among coastal tribes he was held in high esteem. He held his curing rites in what was known as a "spirit house" where all the village gathered.

Unique among the ceremonies of the Northwest was the "potlach" — a Chinook word which meant "to give." A man could show his wealth at such a time and it was a status symbol. Building a house, raising a totem pole, mourning the death of a chief or some other important persons, were some of the reasons to hold a potlach. These events were very dramatic and could be held over a long period of time. There were many songs and dances, great feasts, speeches, and entertainments.

A potlach festivity began in the evening when a dance was given in one of the large dwellings. Honor songs were sung and the host danced alone. One such song had the words, "I am wealthy, that is why I am dancing."

From Cape Flattery in the state of Washington, a Makah mother sings this lullaby:

> *My little son,*
> *You will put a whale harpoon and a sealing spear*
> *into your canoe,*
> *Not knowing what use you will make of them.*

This is one of the first songs a child hears out in that land of the totem-pole makers, where the Indians live by the sea, and are guided and aided by spirit-helpers. The environment and customs of these peoples of the Northwest Coast are very different from those of the other Indian peoples we have described. Since you have read all of this book, it is hoped that you, too, have discovered that all these nations are as different as the nations of other continents over the world.

THE INDIANS AND INDIAN MUSIC TODAY

■ Many of the songs and ceremonies of long ago that have been described in this book are still remembered and performed today. Many of them, however, have been forgotten or are remembered only by the very oldest members of the tribe. The younger Indians do not learn or perform some of the songs and dances because there is little need for them in modern life. Much of the culture of the Indian people has passed away because times have changed, a new way of life has opened, and the old days which needed so many songs and ceremonies do not find a place in today's world.

There are no Buffalo Dances, as in the old days, because the animals are gone and the Indians of the Plains do not hunt them or need them for food. This is one example of the dying-out of an important ceremony that was performed a hundred years ago. Many of the ceremonies, discontinued over the years, have been revived with even more dynamic spirit, and a new faith and renewal of purpose has affected the Indians in many of the tribes. Today there are about 200 tribes and over 400,000 Indians in our country. Very few live in tipis, but most live in modern houses; few ride horseback or walk trails, but most drive cars and trucks for pleasure and work. There are Indians who live on land where the white man decided long ago they must live. As you travel over the country you will pass many Indian reservations. Over the country the Indians have become farmers, miners, construction workers, and teachers. They take part in all professions. You will find them in almost every city in America and probably wouldn't recognize them unless you looked closely. Very few Indians wear buckskin or moccasins. Most of them dress as you do. However, where there is a big gathering, a reunion, or a pow-pow, you will see Indians dressed in their original ceremonial costumes just as some people dress up to go to a party or to church.

A lot of Indians still make native crafts — baskets, silver jewelry, pottery, beadwork — many of them made to sell in shops or as souvenirs. You can often see Indians at festivals and fairs, singing and dancing as in the old days, either to entertain an audience or to demonstrate some of their ancient culture. Indians often appear in movies when stories of pioneer and frontier days are depicted on the screen. Usually they are the enemy.

However, much of the past is still retained among certain Indian tribes. Ceremonies among the Iroquois or the Pueblos, for example, are still held annually just as they always have been. In August every year the rain dances are given in the Southwest, and the Sun Dance is revived as of old among many Plains tribes.

In the past century people other than Indians have taken a great interest in preserving the ancient culture of the tribes. Museums over the country are filled with artifacts and examples of the Indians' past. Recordings have been made of the music of almost every tribe. All these collectors felt that in preserving the past they would help to keep alive, just as many Indians are doing, the traditions and culture of the first singing Americans.

READING LIST FOR STUDENTS

FELDMAN, SUSAN, ed., *The Story Telling Stone — Myths and Tales of the American Indian.* New York, Dell, 1965.

HOFMANN, CHARLES, *War Whoops and Medicine Songs.* Boston, Boston Music Co., 1952.

HOFSINDE, ROBERT, *The Indian Medicine Man.* New York, Morrow, 1966.

————, *The Indian's Secret World.* New York, Morrow, 1955.

SALOMON, JULIAN HARRIS, *The Book of Indian Crafts and Indian Lore.* New York, Harper and Row, 1928.

STIRLING, MATTHEW, ed., *Indians of the Americas.* Washington, The National Geographic Society, 1961.

READING LIST FOR TEACHERS AND PARENTS

CARTER, E. RUSSELL, *The Gift Is Rich.* New York, Friendship Press, 1955. (Also in paperback.)

COLLIER, JOHN, *Indians of the Americas.* New York, Mentor Books, 1948.

DENSMORE, FRANCES, *The American Indians and Their Music.* New York, The Woman's Press, 1936.

————, *Bulletins* on music of American Indians issued by the Bureau of American Ethnology, Smithsonian Institution, Washington, D. C., especially *Chippewa Music* (1910, 1913), and *Teton Sioux Music* (1918), available in libraries.

DRIVER, HAROLD E., *Indians of North America.* Chicago, University of Chicago Press, 1961.

FERGUSSON, ERNA, *Dancing Gods — Indian Ceremonials of New Mexico and Arizona.* Albuquerque, University of New Mexico Press, 1931.

SPENCER, ROBERT F., *et al, The Native Americans.* New York, Harper and Row, 1965.

UNDERHILL, RUTH MURRAY, *Red Man's America,* Chicago, University of Chicago Press, 1953.

————, *Red Man's Religion.* Chicago, University of Chicago Press, 1965.

■ The recording in the back of this book includes seven examples of Indian songs representing seven tribes. These demonstrate types of Indian singing as well as some of the musical instruments discussed in previous pages. The brief examples may stimulate interest in hearing the complete songs or additional portions of certain ceremonies. The record is offered to serve as encouragement to additional study and to make the listener aware of the variety found in this music.

Excerpts on this recording come from several collectors. A listing of available recordings, from which these excerpts were taken, follows:

1. *Buffalo Dance* (Kiowa)
   Collected by Willard Rhodes, from Archive of American Folksong (AAFS) L 36.
2. *Snake Ceremony* (Hopi)
   Collected by Jesse Walter Fewkes, from early recording, originally Gennett Recording Company. Excerpt also to be found on Folkways FE 4394.
3. *False Face Society* (Iroquois)
   Collected by William N. Fenton, from AAFS L 6.
4. *Flute Melody* (Chippewa)
   Collected by Charles Hofmann, from Library of Congress collection. Also on Folkways FE 4381.
5. *Sun Dance* (Sioux)
   Collected by Willard Rhodes, from AAFS L 40.
6. *Lullaby* (Zuni)
   Collected by Charles Hofmann, from Library of Congress collection. Also on Folkways FE 4381.
7. *Deer Dance* (Yaqui)
   Collected by Henrietta Yurchenco, from AAFS L 19, with additional material on Folkways FE 4413.

OTHER RECORDINGS OF INDIAN MUSIC

A CHILD'S INTRODUCTION TO THE AMERICAN INDIAN
   Chief Red Thundercloud and company with commentary and songs.
   (Micmac, Catawba, Seneca, Creek, Cheyenne)
   Prestige-International 13076

DANCES OF THE NORTH AMERICAN INDIANS
   Compiled and edited by Ronnie and Stu Lipner.
   (Navaho, Sioux, Apache, San Ildefonso, Zuni, Flathead, Canadian Plains)
   Folkways FD 6510

HEALING SONGS OF THE AMERICAN INDIANS
   Recorded by Frances Densmore, selected and edited by Charles Hofmann.
   (Chippewa, Sioux, Yuma, Northern Ute, Papago, Menominee)
   Folkways FE 4251

HOPI KATCINA SONGS, with other Hopi chants
   Recorded by Jesse Walter Fewkes, edited by Charles Hofmann.
   Folkways FE 4394

INDIAN MUSIC OF THE SOUTHWEST
   Recorded by Laura C. Boulton.
   (Hopi, Zuni, Navaho, Taos, San Ildefonso, Santa Ana, Mohave, Papago, Pima,
   Apache)
   Folkways FW 8850

MUSIC OF THE AMERICAN INDIANS SOUTHWEST
   Recorded by Willard Rhodes.
   (Taos, San Ildefonso, Zuni, Hopi, Navaho, Western Apache, Yuma, Walapai, Papa-
   go, Havasupai)
   Folkways FE 4420

MUSIC OF THE SIOUX AND NAVAHO
   Recorded by Willard Rhodes.
   Folkways FE 4401

SENECA SONGS FROM COLDSPRING LONGHOUSE
   Recorded by William N. Fenton.
   Library of Congress AAFS L 17

SONGS OF THE IROQUOIS LONGHOUSE
   Recorded by William N. Fenton.
   Library of Congress AAFS L 6

WAR WHOOPS AND MEDICINE SONGS
   Recorded by Charles Hofmann.
   (Winnebago, Zuni, Acoma, Oglala Sioux, Chippewa)
   Folkways FE 4381

MUSIC OF THE PUEBLOS, APACHE AND NAVAHO
   Edited by Donald Nelson Brown.
   Taylor Museum of the Colorado Springs Fine Arts Center, Matrix KCMS 1204-5

INDIAN MUSIC OF THE CANADIAN PLAINS
   Recorded by Ken Peacock.
   (Cree, Assiboine, Blood, Blackfoot) Folkways FE 4464

SONGS AND DANCES OF THE FLATHEAD INDIANS
   Recorded by Alan P. Merriam.
   Folkways FE 4445

SONGS AND DANCES OF GREAT LAKES INDIANS
   Recorded by Gertrude Prokasch Kurath.
   (Ottawa, Ojibwa; Iroquois: Onondaga, Cayuga-Tutelo, Onondago-Tuscarora)
   Folkways Monograph Series 4003

NAVAHO CREATION CHANTS
   Recorded by David P. McAlester, sung by Hosteen Klah.
   Peabody Museum, Harvard University, five 10-inch discs, 78 rpm.

MUSIC OF THE PAWNEE
   Recorded by Dr. Gene Weltfish, sung by Mark Evarts.
   Folkways FE 4334

DANCE AND WAR SONGS OF THE KIOWA INDIANS
   Recorded by J. Gordon Thornton.
   Folkways FE 4393

SONGS OF THE SEMINOLE INDIANS OF FLORIDA
   Recorded by Frances Densmore, selected and edited by Charles Hofmann.
   Folkways FE 4383

THE SMITHSONIAN-DENSMORE COLLECTION at the Library of Congress, Archive of Folklore:

SONGS OF THE CHIPPEWA, recorded 1907–1910. (AAFS L 16)

SONGS OF THE MENOMINEE, MANDAN AND HIDATSA, 1915–1929. (AAFS L 33)

SONGS OF THE NOOTKA AND QUILEUTE, 1923 & 1926. (AAFS L 32)

SONGS OF THE PAPAGO, 1920. (AAFS L 31)

SONGS OF THE PAWNEE; SONGS OF THE NORTHERN UTE, 1914–1920. (AAFS L 25)

SONGS OF THE SIOUX, 1911–1914. (AAFS L 23)

SONGS OF THE YUMA, COCOPA AND YAQUI, 1922. (AAFS L 24)

MUSIC OF THE AMERICAN INDIAN, a series recorded and edited by Willard Rhodes in co-
   operation with the Bureau of Indian Affairs and the Indian Arts and Crafts Board.
   Library of Congress, Archive of Folklore.
   Vol. 1: *Northwest (Puget Sound)* (AAFS L 34)
   Vol. 2: *Kiowa* (AAFS L 35)
   Vol. 3: *Indian Songs of Today* (Seminole, Creek, Potawatomi, Sioux, Navaho,
   Tewa, Picuris Pueblo, San Jun Pueblo, Kiowa, Cherokee, Tlingit) (AAFS L 36)

ABOUT THE AUTHOR

■   Charles Hofmann has pursued an interest in folk music since his early years, first collecting it and later teaching and lecturing about it. He was a student of Dr. Curt Sachs in music history and of Dr. Frances Densmore of the Smithsonian Institution in American Indian music. He collected folk material among fourteen Indian groups for the library of Congress, and made recordings of songs of twenty nationality groups. He has lectured at the American Museum of Natural History and at other museums, colleges, and libraries in many parts of the United States on primitive, Oriental, and folk music. He has originated radio programs and edited record albums.